Tactics

Tactics
U.S. Marines Corps

FMFM 1-3

GOVERNMENT REPRINTS PRESS
Washington, D.C.

© Ross & Perry, Inc. 2001 All rights reserved.

No claim to U.S. government work contained throughout this book.

Protected under the Berne Convention. Published 2001

Printed in The United States of America
Ross & Perry, Inc. Publishers
717 Second St., N.E., Suite 200
Washington, D.C. 20002
Telephone (202) 675-8300
Facsimile (202) 675-8400
info@RossPerry.com

SAN 253-8555

Government Reprints Press Edition 2001

Government Reprints Press is an Imprint of Ross & Perry, Inc.

Library of Congress Control Number: 2001092429

http://www.GPOreprints.com

ISBN 1-931641-16-1

The paper used in this publication meets the requirements for permanence established by the American National Standard for Information Sciences "Permanence of Paper for Printed Library Materials" (ANSI Z39.48-1984).

All rights reserved. No copyrighted part of this publication may be reproduced, stored in a retrieval system, or transmitted, in any form or by any means, electronic, photocopying, recording, or otherwise, without the prior written permission of the publisher.

DEPARTMENT OF THE NAVY
Headquarters United States Marine Corps
Washington, D.C. 20380-0001

1 June 1991

FOREWORD

This book is about winning in combat. Winning in combat requires many things: excellence in techniques, understanding of the battlefield, an appreciation of the opponent, exemplary leadership, battlefield judgment, and combat power. Yet these factors by themselves are no indicator of probable success in battle. Our study of history unveils that many armies, both winners and losers, possessed many or all of these attributes. When we examine closely the differences between victor and vanquished, we draw one prevailing conclusion. This is that success went to the armies whose leaders, senior and junior, could best harmonize their efforts — their skills and their assets — toward a decisive end. Their success arose not from techniques, procedures, and material but from their leaders' abilities to uniquely and effectively combine them. What they share in common is an uncommon approach to combat. Then as now, winning in combat depends upon leaders — tactical leaders — who can think creatively and act decisively.

This manual is designed for all tactical leaders. Its content pertains equally to all Marine leaders, whether their duties entail combat service support, combat support, or combat arms. It applies to the MAGTF commander as well as the squadron commander and the fire team leader. Every Marine faces tactical decisions in battle regardless of his role.

The concepts and principles within this manual are battle-tested. During Operation Desert Storm, our success on the battlefield resulted directly from the military skill of our leaders at every level of command. Because of their tactical skill and battlefield judgment, our commanders shaped the battlefield and applied the available means of warfare, achieving the tactical and operational advantage at the decisive time and place. We must remember that, although our equipment was superior to that of our enemy, the professionalism of our leaders and warriors won our decisive victory.

Tactics is consonant with FMFM 1, *Warfighting*, and FMFM 1-1 *Campaigning*. It presumes an understanding of the warfighting philosophy, applying it specifically to the tactical level. Like FMFM 1, it is not prescriptive but descriptive, providing guidance in the form of concepts and values. This manual illustrates a philosophy for waging and winning combat.

A. M. GRAY
General, U.S. Marine Corps
Commandant of the Marine Corps

DISTRIBUTION: 139 000104 00

Tactics

Introduction

Chapter 1. Achieving a Decision
Antietam – Cannae – Understanding Decisiveness – How to Achieve a Decision – Conceptualizing the Battlefield – Coup d'Oeil – The Focus of Effort – Intent and Mission – Summary

Chapter 2. Gaining Leverage
Leverage – Asymmetry – Ambush – Maneuver – Building on Advantage – Summary

Chapter 3. Trapping the Enemy
A New Order – Pincers – Combined Arms – Surprise – Uncertainty and Deception – Summary

Chapter 4. Moving Faster
Speed in Combat – What Is Speed? – Speed and Time – Timing – Relative Speed – Continuous Speed – Speed and Change – Becoming Faster – Summary

Chapter 5. Cooperating

Control in Combat? — Cooperation — Discipline — Summary

Chapter 6. Making It Happen

Training — Education — Professional Reading and Historical Study — Exercises — Competition — Critiques — Summary

Notes

Introduction

"There is only one principle of war and that's this. Hit the other fellow, as quick as you can, and as hard as you can, where it hurts him the most, when he ain't looking." [1]

WHAT IS TACTICS?

All Marines know what tactics is. After all, we've heard people talking about tactics since our first days in recruit training or Officer Candidates School. Most of us probably recall encountering tactics even before becoming Marines. People talk about chess tactics, tennis tactics, running tactics, tactics for studying and for getting better grades, etc.

So what **is** tactics? This isn't just a rhetorical question. Think for a minute of what tactics means to you. How would you define it? . . .

Perhaps you just found that defining tactics isn't quite as simple as it appears. A formal definition of tactics appears in Joint Pub 1-02. It says tactics is "the employment of units in combat . . . the ordered arrangement and maneuver of units in relation to each other and/or to the enemy in order to utilize their full potentialities." Although an official definition, it is merely a starting point. Our inquiry should not stop there. Over the centuries even great military leaders and thinkers have found it difficult to say exactly what tactics is. Each attempt offers a somewhat different perspective:

" . . . *proper means of organization and action to give unity to effort* . . ."[2]

—Du Picq

"... the changeable element in warfare."[3]
—Palit

"... the art of leading troops in combat."[4]
—Von der Goltz

"... the theory and use of military forces in combat."[5]
—Clausewitz

"... the art of fighting."[6]
—Montgomery

"... "the art of executing the designs of strategy."[7]
—Wheeler

"... the art and science of winning engagements and battles. It includes the use of firepower and maneuver, the integration of different arms, and the immediate exploitation of success to defeat the enemy . . . the product of judgment and creativity . . ."[8]
—FMFM 1

FMFM 1-3 ——————————— Introduction

A DEFINITION OF TACTICS

This last quotation is the Marine Corps' approach toward tactics. It is Marine Corps doctrine. What does it tell us?

First, it recognizes that tactics is neither purely art nor purely science, but rather the product of the two elements, each of which multiplies the other. We cannot simply add "judgment and creativity" (art), to "techniques and procedures" (science) and arrive at a sum which is tactics. Rather, we use each to increase manyfold the value of the others.

Second, it says that tactics is about "winning engagements and battles." Whereas the conduct of campaigns (operations) and wars (strategy) implies broad dimensions of time and space, engagements and battles involve fighting and defeating an enemy at more narrowly defined times and places.

Third, tactics relies upon the use of firepower, movement, and the integration of different arms, which is to say combined arms. Modern tactics is combined arms tactics.

Finally, a single tactical success is not an end in itself. Tactics must serve a greater purpose *beyond* winning the engagement or battle. Through "immediate exploitation of success," tactical actions yield operational gains.

Marine Tactics

This, then, is tactics. But is it all we can say on the subject that would be of use to Marines? As Marines, we have distinct characteristics. First, we may specialize in one of three basic areas—ground, aviation, or combat service support—which are three of the four basic components of every Marine Air-Ground Task Force (MAGTF). Second, regardless of that specialization, we all fight together as one single whole, as a MAGTF. So we need to think about tactics in ways that relate to each separate specialty (combat service support, ground, and aviation), but do so *in ways that relate each to the others* by showing what they share—their common tactical ground.

That is what this book attempts to do. It is not a book about fighter tactics, or infantry tactics, or tactics for emergency field repair of combat equipment. It is about tactics for all of these things and more. It is a book of shared tactical concepts, common to all Marines in all our many skills and specialties.

Of course, you must apply these ideas according to the situation. With them, you can face any situation with a useful frame of reference common to all Marines. That brings us back to our definition of tactics from FMFM 1. As that definition notes, the purpose of tactics is winning. That is also the purpose of this book: to show all Marines some tactical concepts which can help us win.

Chapter 1

Achieving a Decision

"Combat situations cannot be solved by rule. The art of war has no traffic with rules, for the infinitely varied circumstances and conditions of combat never produce exactly the same situation twice. Mission, terrain, weather, dispositions, armament, morale, supply, and comparative strength are variables whose mutations always combine to form a new tactical pattern. Thus, in battle, each situation is unique and must be solved on its own merits."

"It follows, then, that the leader who would become a competent tactician must first close his mind to the alluring formulae that well-meaning people offer in the name of victory. To master his difficult art he must learn to cut to the heart of a situation, recognize its decisive elements and base his course of action on these." [1]

FMFM 1-3 ——————————— Achieving a Decision

The first basic concept in tactics is achieving a decision. This concept marks a major change from the customary American way of war. In the past, American forces have generally sought incremental gains: taking a hill here or a town there, pushing the FEBA[2] forward a few kilometers, or adding to the body count. This attitude was consistent with attrition warfare, which sees war as a slow, cumulative process. In contrast, tactics in maneuver warfare always aim at achieving a decision. What do we mean by achieving a decision?

ANTIETAM

On September 17, 1862, General Robert E. Lee's Confederate Army of Northern Virginia fought the Union Army of the Potomac under Major General George B. McClellan in the vicinity of Antietam Creek, near Sharpsburg, Maryland. Lee's Maryland campaign had begun on September 4, when his army crossed the Potomac River, entered Maryland, and invaded Northern soil for the first time.

On September 16, both armies massed near Sharpsburg. McClellan initially enjoyed an almost 4:1 advantage in infantrymen but did not attack. By midday General T.J. "Stonewall" Jackson's corps arrived from Harper's Ferry, but the Union still had an advantage of slightly over 2:1. Again, McClellan did not attack. Outnumbered, with his back to the Potomac, Lee constructed defensive works.

At dawn on the 17th, General Joseph Hooker advanced his three Union divisions, with orders to assault the Confederate left. So began the savage fighting which remains the single bloodiest day in American military history — Antietam. Union and Confederate forces mauled one another in three essentially separate engagements. Twenty thousand Union infantrymen, over two divisions, were never committed. Combined casualties were nearly 4,000 dead, 17,000 wounded, and 2,000 missing. The Union suffered the lion's share.

The battle did not resume on the 18th, each force waiting for the other to move. That evening the Army of Northern Virginia recrossed the Potomac River into Virginia. Although he retained a fully rested, combat-effective force of 20,000, McClellan did not pursue. The starving, exhausted, and ill-equipped Army of Northern Virginia was not defeated or destroyed. It withdrew to rebuild and fight Union forces on many other battlefields. Antietam was not decisive.[3]

What commentators mean when they call the combat at Antietam Creek *indecisive* is that it had *no result* beyond many dead and wounded American soldiers, Northern and Southern. It had no meaningful effect. Lincoln implored McClellan to "not let him [the Confederates] get off without being hurt." In reply, McClellan promised to "send trophies"; however, all the commander in chief received was casualty lists and a prolonged war.

Some might argue that Antietam contributed to the ultimate Union victory because the Union could replace its losses more easily than the Confederacy. In a narrow sense, this is correct. Yet it reflects the attrition concept of incremental gains through *body counts*. Attrition warfare can lead to victory, but the cost is usually terrible—as the Civil War showed. The Marine Corps' doctrine of maneuver warfare is not satisfied to call an incremental gain a success. It demands a decision.

CANNAE

On August 2, 216 B.C., the Carthaginian general Hannibal fought the Roman army under Varro near the city of Cannae.

As dawn broke, Hannibal drew up his force of 50,000 veterans with his left flank anchored on the River Aufidus, secured from envelopment by the more numerous Romans. His center contained only a thin line of infantry; his main force was concentrated on the flanks. His left and right wings each contained deep phalanxes of heavy infantry. Eight thousand cavalry tied the left of his line to the river. Two thousand cavalry protected his open right flank. Eight thousand men guarded his camp in the rear.

Varro and more than 80,000 Romans accepted the challenge. Seeing the well-protected Carthaginian flanks, Varro dismissed any attempt to envelop. He decided instead to crush his opponent by sheer weight of numbers. He placed 65,000 men in his center, 2,400 cavalry on his right, and 4,800 cavalry on his left and sent 11,000 men to attack the Carthaginian camp.

Following preliminary skirmishes, Hannibal moved his light center line forward into a salient against the Roman center. Then, his heavy cavalry on the left crushed the opposing Roman cavalry and swung completely around the Roman rear. The Roman cavalry fled the field.

The Carthaginian heavy cavalry next turned against the rear of the dense Roman infantry who were pressing Hannibal's thin center line. At the same time, Hannibal wheeled his right and left wings into the flanks of the Roman center. The Romans were boxed in, unable to maneuver or use their weapons effectively. Between 50,000 and 60,000 Romans died that day, and the Roman army was destroyed. At the tactical level, Hannibal's victory was decisive.

Understanding Decisiveness

What do these examples tell us about achieving a decision?

First, they tell us that achieving a decision is important. An indecisive battle wastes the lives of those who fight and die in it. It wastes the efforts of the living as well. All the wounds and pain, the sweat and striving, the equipment destroyed or used up, the supplies expended—all are for little. They bring no great result; they have no further meaning, except comparative attrition and perhaps an incremental gain.

Second, achieving a decision is not easy. History is littered with indecisive battles. Few of the commanders who fought them sought deliberately to avoid a decision. Sometimes the enemy kept them from achieving the decision they sought. In other cases, they were unable to think through how to make the battle decisive. In still other cases—far too many—the commanders had no concept of seeking a decisive result. They fought a battle because it was there to fight; they had no notion of a larger result.

That leads to the third lesson our examples point out. To be decisive, a battle or an engagement must lead to a result beyond itself. Within a battle, an action that is decisive must lead directly to winning the battle as a whole. **For the battle as a whole to be decisive, it must lead directly to winning the campaign—to an operational success.** Similarly, a decisive campaign must lead directly to strategic victory. A battle like that fought at Antietam was indecisive because it had no larger result. It had no meaning beyond the blood-soaked ground and the rows of dead.

How to Achieve a Decision

Once you understand what is meant by the term *decisive* and why it is important always to seek a decision, a question naturally arises: How do you do it?

Conceptualizing the Battlefield

There is no easy answer to that question because each battle will have its own unique answer. As with so much in warfare, it depends on the situation. No formula or process or acronym can give you the answer.

FMFM 1-3 ——————————— Achieving a Decision

Rather, the answer lies in military judgment, in the ability of the commander to conceptualize the battlefield and to act decisively. This is the first and greatest duty of a commander at any level: he must picture in his own mind how he intends to fight the battle. He must think through what he wants to do—what result he wants from his actions, and how he will get that result. Central to his thinking must be the question, "In this situation, what result will be decisive?" He must ask himself this question not just once but constantly, as the battle progresses. As the situation changes, so will the answer and the actions that derive from it.

We can see a good example of conceptualizing the battle so that it leads to a decision in General Robert E. Lee's approach to the battle of Chancellorsville. Despite Union pontoon bridges thrown across the Rappahannock River at Fredericksburg, Virginia, General Lee foresaw that a battle at this location would merely be a Union holding action. Further, any Confederate attempt to stem a Union river crossing would mean fighting under Union artillery which dominated the town from the heights across the river. Thus, Fredericksburg itself was not a promising place for the Confederates to achieve a decision.

General Lee predicted that the Union main effort would be against the center of the Confederate line, arrayed northwest of Fredericksburg. Leaving minimum forces in the city itself to protect his right flank, he reinforced his units already in the vicinity of Chancellorsville, contrary even to the counsel of his trusted "Stonewall" Jackson.

After sending engineers forward to reconnoiter the Union center, General Lee confirmed his prediction: The Union positions at the center were too strong to assault. Having ruled out a Union attack to his right because of open terrain, and confirming no opening at his center, Lee considered what could be done on his left. Here, he determined to move a force around the Union right flank by way of concealed routes and to attack the Union rear. He put General Jackson to the task. Jackson's flanking march and attack at Chancellorsville unravelled the Union line and sent the Union forces reeling back across the Rapidan River. General Lee's ability to conceptualize the battlefield guided him in striking the Union forces at the decisive point.

COUP D'OEIL

At Chancellorsville, General Lee showed the quality which 18th century military pundits viewed as most important for any commander: *coup d'oeil* (pronounced koo doy). It means literally "strike of the eye." *Coup d'oeil* is the ability to look at a military situation and immediately see its essence, especially the key enemy weakness or weaknesses which, if exploited, can lead to a decision.[4] We see this ability in history's great captains, in people like Alexander, Frederick the Great, and

FMFM 1-3 ——————————— Achieving a Decision

Napoleon. It is largely what made them great captains—what enabled them, in battle after battle, to achieve decisive results.

Napoleon demonstrated *coup d'oeil* in his recapture of Toulon in 1793. After just a quick look at the situation, he saw that the key to victory lay in isolating Toulon from the seaward as well as the landward side. That could be accomplished by placing artillery on a promontory that overlooked the harbor. The English held the promontory on which they had built a large, imposing earthwork known as Fort Mulgrave. Napoleon focused his effort, especially his artillery, on Fort Mulgrave with the result that it fell in the first hours of the French assault on December 17. By midday on the 18th, the French had a battery of ten guns on the promontory prepared to sweep the harbor. The British fleet was forced to evacuate.[5]

Coup d'oeil is the inspiration—the hunch—upon which a leader begins to conceptualize the battle. How does he translate that vision into action?

The Focus of Effort

The first and most important answer reflects one of the central concepts of maneuver warfare: You achieve a decision by focusing your efforts. The focus of effort is the *commander's bid to achieve a decision*. As he thinks about the battle, he determines, as best he can tell beforehand, what action will be decisive. Then, he designates a unit to perform that action. This is his focus of effort.

The focus of effort is the concept that makes maneuver warfare decisive. Maneuver means much more than forces rapidly moving around the battlefield with no intention of bringing force to bear on the enemy. Maneuver is the combination of movement and fire to gain an advantage on the enemy. The focus of effort ties together all the maneuvering and points it at the enemy so that Marines will win. Without a focus of effort, combat would quickly break down into a multitude of unrelated actions, each divergent from the others. With a focus of effort, you have a multitude of independent but related actions, each convergent with the others. Along with the commander's intent and the mission, the focus of effort is the glue that holds maneuver warfare together. And it does more than that: It hurls those many maneuvering elements against the enemy's key weakness.

The focus of effort is the commander's bid to achieve a decision; he works to ensure all his forces and assets support it. Sometimes, he may use them to support it directly. For example, he may give it all his air support, even all his artillery support. He may concentrate his reserve in echelon behind it. He may give it all his antitank or antiair weapons. Often, he will have to take substantial risks elsewhere in order to give his focus of effort the greatest possible punch.

In other situations, some actions may support the focus of effort indirectly. For example, a commander may use his aviation in an attempt to deceive, to lead the enemy to think his focus is other than where it really is. Aviation is particularly useful for this because it can concentrate to support the real focus more quickly than ground forces.

The Germans used their aviation this way at the beginning of their French campaign in 1940. On May 10, "by scattering their bombing across a broad area, they hoped to conceal their intentions to make their main attack across eastern Belgium and toward Sedan and to make the French think the main effort was taking place in northern and central Belgium." Yet, just three days later, on May 13, they had 310 medium bombers, 200 dive bombers, and 200 fighters over Sedan. They used the ability of aviation to drop its deception role quickly and focus its effort at the decisive point.[6]

While a commander always has a focus of effort, he may alter it during the course of a battle as events unfold. The enemy is unpredictable, and few battles flow exactly as the commander had originally conceived. He must adjust, and one way to do so is by changing the focus of effort. For example, if, in an attack by a Marine Expeditionary Force, 2d Marines were designated the focus of effort but ran into heavy enemy resistance while the adjacent 7th Marines made a breakthrough, the ground combat element commander would probably redesignate 7th Marines as the focus of effort. This new designation must not, however, be merely nominal. It means that all the combat power which was originally directed to support 2d Marines now goes to 7th Marines.

Central to the ability to defeat enemies more numerous than oneself, focus of effort enables you to have greater combat power at the decisive point. That decision—deciding what unit would be the focus and why, then making it real by ruthlessly concentrating combat power in support of it— is a test of a commander's character. Field Marshal Paul von Hindenburg said that an operation without a focus is like a man without character.[7]

The focus of effort is the main and most important answer to the question, "How do you achieve a decision?" However, it is an answer that immediately raises another question: "How do I focus my effort?"

FMFM 1-3 —————————— Achieving a Decision

INTENT AND MISSION

From the commander's concept of how he will fight and win the battle comes not only his focus of effort, but also his intent and the missions he assigns his subordinates.

The commander's intent describes the result he wants to get from the battle and his general concept of how he will get it. It gives his subordinates a clear understanding of what is in his mind—his mental picture of the battle. The result is especially important because the battle will often develop in ways he could not anticipate. His concept of how he will get the result he wants may therefore change. But as long as his subordinates clearly understand the end result he wants, they can adapt to changing circumstances on their own without risking a diffusion of effort.

The commander's intent seems to be a simple concept. Yet, in practice, many people have difficulty with it. Often the difficulty stems from the fact that the commander does not have a clear mental picture of either the result he wants or how, in general terms, he thinks he can get it. Consequently, the commander's intent is either empty of content, like "Defeat the enemy," or focuses inward on process, like "Use initiative and boldness," rather than outward on the enemy and the situation.

Remember, the commander's intent tells you <u>what is in the commander's mind</u>. A commander's intent that is empty or procedural is of no value to subordinates in terms of how to fight and win the battle.

Once the commander has a clear concept of the battle in his mind, he then has a responsibility to convey it clearly to his subordinates. In doing this, the form of the order is unimportant. It may be oral or written; it may be short and to the point with little or no adherence to any set format. Again, it is the result that is important: <u>the subordinates' understanding of what is in the commander's mind</u>. The means should be flexible so that they can be adapted to the situation and to the people involved. The words needed to convey the intent clearly to one subordinate may be different from the words needed with another subordinate. Generally, clarity is easiest to achieve in face-to-face meetings.

From the commander's intent comes the subordinate unit's mission. The mission is in effect a slice of the overall intent, <u>the result the commander wants from that particular unit</u>. The subordinate needs to know both the mission and the intent so that he understands how the result he is to obtain fits into the result wanted from the battle. Again, that understanding is of key importance in allowing the subordinate to adapt to changing circumstances while keeping his effort focused and ensuring it supports and complements the efforts of other friendly units.

Once the commander has made certain his subordinates understand his intent, their missions, and the focus of effort, he should generally give them maximum latitude in deciding **how** to accomplish their mission and get the result their superior desires. If the **how** is dictated to them in detail, they will be unable to adapt to the rapid change that is characteristic of combat. They will miss taking advantage of fleeting opportunities, and they will be unable to respond to dangers that appear suddenly and unexpectedly. In short, they will be rigid and ineffective.

In many respects, the heart of maneuver warfare is telling the subordinate what result is needed, then leaving it up to him to obtain the result however he thinks best. That is why maneuver warfare is also called mission tactics.

SUMMARY

As a leader, whether of a fire team or a Marine Expeditionary Force, you are responsible for results. In combat, the most important result is a decisive victory. To get it, you must work ceaselessly in peacetime to develop in yourself a talent for *coup d'oeil* and for thinking through how you are going to win whatever battle you face. You must learn how to translate that mental picture into a focus of effort, a statement of intent, and missions for your subordinates.

Finally, in all your relations with your subordinates, you must learn how to make crystal clear to them the results you want—the output—while leaving it to them to determine methods—the input. Only in this manner can you hope to have the speed and agility in your unit that maneuver warfare requires.

Chapter 2

Gaining Leverage

"*I served over 31 years' active duty with the Marine Corps, saw combat in both Korea and Vietnam, and attended service schools from the Basic School to the National War College. Yet only toward the end of my military career did I realize how little I really understood the art of war. Even as a PFC in Korea, after being medevaced along with most of my platoon after a fruitless frontal assault against superior North Korean forces, it seemed to me there had to be a better way to wage war. Seventeen years later, commanding a battalion at Khe Sanh, I was resolved that none of my Marines would die for lack of superior combat power. But we were still relying on the concentration of superior firepower to win—essentially still practicing Grant's attrition warfare. And we were still doing frontal assaults!*"[1]

FMFM 1-3 — Gaining Leverage

Many Marines are poker players. When you play poker, you often try to control the expression on your face so as to mislead your opponents. We call that a poker face, and you often use it to bluff. You use it to gain a *decisive advantage*, one that does not come simply from the strength of the cards you hold. That is leverage.

Leverage

Many Marines study martial arts. A major principle of most martial arts is using the opponent's strength and momentum against him. Again, this gains a decisive advantage; it gives you more force than your muscles can provide. That is leverage.

Leverage through a decisive advantage is our next tactical concept. It runs through all tactics.

A light infantry force draws an enemy armored force into rugged, wooded terrain. Unable to see more than a couple hundred yards and restricted to moving on roads, the tanks are easy targets for infantrymen who remain invisible. The infantry destroys the armor by gaining a decisive advantage through terrain.

An attack aircraft flies at treetop level, hugging the earth's contour. Recognizing the upcoming bluffs on his right as his reference point, the pilot pops the aircraft into a vertical climb to locate the enemy column at his 11 o'clock. He quickly rolls in to strafe and rocket the enemy vehicles. Despite enemy air defenses, the pilot destroys several vehicles and stalls the enemy convoy. By flying at an extremely low level and climbing quickly, the pilot evaded the enemy's air defenses. Neither radar nor shoulder-launched antiair weapons could acquire a target. The pilot attacked with a decisive advantage.

A Marine Air-Ground Task Force, using a mechanized force and deep air support, successfully penetrates the enemy's forward defenses and immediately exploits the breakthrough. As the force enters the enemy's support areas, it encounters extensive minefields. Few tanks and vehicles are destroyed, but many lose tracks and roadwheels, and the exploitation is threatened. As these mobility kills mount, momentum lessens. However, combat maintenance teams, traveling with the penetrating force, quickly repair the salvageable vehicles. The MAGTF recovers enough lost vehicles to restore its momentum and turns the exploitation into a pursuit, completely routing the enemy force. Marines gained a decisive advantage by being able to return vehicles to service as fast as the enemy could disable them.

FMFM 1-3 ——————————— **Gaining Leverage**

Each of these cases illustrates leverage, or decisive advantage. Too often in history, people have thought of war as a jousting contest between medieval knights where rules put each knight on an equal basis. All they were allowed to do was charge head-on at each other. Like all sports, jousting was carefully designed to be fair.

In war, however, we shouldn't play at jousting. Victory goes to the side that fights smart. Creating and making use of decisive advantages is central to modern tactics. What are some ways you can gain leverage through decisive advantages?

ASYMMETRY

A common element in most cases of leverage is asymmetry. Think of a lever: its power comes from the fact that the fulcrum is not equidistant from the ends of the lever. The two arms of the lever are asymmetrical, and by putting force on the longer side, you get leverage.

The same is true of war. Considering a war in Europe, one Soviet specialist was questioned concerning the Soviet answer to the superiority of the U.S. Air Force's F-15 fighter. He replied that the answer was not another Soviet fighter; it was putting a T-72 tank on the U.S. Air Force's runway. That is asymmetry.

Fighting asymmetrically is not simply a matter of countering enemy forces with unlike forces: aircraft against tank or infantry against armor. Asymmetry also depends upon tactics that use the enemy's weaknesses as leverage. When an infantry force encounters an enemy infantry force entrenched in a linear defense, its leaders need not call tanks forward to apply asymmetry. Attacks by penetration and infiltration are asymmetrical tactics. Instead of attacking frontally, the infantry commander seeks to avoid the enemy's linear strength by either filtering forces through the defensive position for a follow-on attack (infiltration) or by concentrating his efforts on a very narrow front (penetration). He gains leverage by avoiding the preponderance of enemy combat power dispersed across a wide front.

AMBUSH

Perhaps the most common tactical tool for gaining leverage and a decisive advantage is the ambush. All Marines are familiar with an ambush as a type of combat patrol. In maneuver warfare, ambush takes on a much broader meaning, and the *ambush mentality* runs through all tactics.

The ambush mentality is probably not new to you. You may know the ambush mentality from sports. In football, the trap block is an ambush. You pull an offensive lineman off the line, leaving a hole. When a defender comes through the hole, another lineman suddenly blocks him from the side, usually knocking him down. You blind-side him. That is the ambush mentality.

In basketball, setting up a pick is an ambush. As your teammate drives to the basket, you step into the defender's path from behind, blocking his path, stopping his defense, and momentarily clearing a new lane to the basket. Again, that is the ambush mentality.

The ambush mentality tries to turn every situation into an ambush. In this broader sense, an ambush has several distinct qualities.

First, in an ambush you try to *surprise the enemy*. Think of a patrol that you ambush. They are walking through the woods when suddenly, out of nowhere, they are under fire from every direction. Probably they are taking heavy casualties. In addition, their thinking may be paralyzed. The psychological effect of surprise has a quality all its own. To have an ambush mentality means that you always try to surprise the enemy, to do the unexpected. Surprise is the rule rather than the exception.

Second, you want to *draw your enemy unknowingly into a trap*. This will often involve deceiving him. You make one course of action appear inviting when, in fact, that is just where you want him to come because you are waiting for him.

Third, an ambush is *invisible*. If the ambush is not invisible, it ceases to be an ambush and becomes a target. On the modern battlefield, if you can be seen, you can be destroyed. Whether you are defending or attacking, the enemy must not see you until it is too late, until he is falling to your fires. Surprise often depends upon invisibility.

The reverse slope defense is an example of using invisibility to spring an ambush. The enemy does not know you are there until he comes over the crest of a hill and is hit by your fires. His vehicles are hit on their soft underbellies. His troops stand fully exposed to your weapons. Because he could not see you until the last moment, he could not plaster you with artillery fire. The reverse slope not only protects you from his fire; it protects you from his observation. That is the ambush mentality: *do not let yourself be seen.*

Fourth, in an ambush you want to *shock the enemy*. Instead of taking him under fire gradually with a few weapons at long range, you wait until he is within easy range of every weapon. You then open up suddenly, all at once, with everything you've got. He is paralyzed, at least for a time, by the shock. He cannot react. Everything was going fine, no enemy seemed to be anywhere around, and suddenly he is in a firestorm with people falling all around him. Often, he will panic, making his problem worse.

Finally, in the ambush mentality, you *always focus on the enemy*. The purpose of an ambush is not to hold a piece of terrain. It is to destroy the enemy. You use terrain to effect the ambush, but terrain is not what you are fighting for.

Maneuver

Gaining a decisive advantage is what maneuver is all about. Fighting by rules and checklists leads to linear defenses and frontal attacks. As you know, frontal attacks and linear defenses tend to be indecisive. To attain a decision, you need a decisive advantage, and you often get it by maneuvering.

What do we think of when we say "maneuver"? The classical view of maneuver is movement in combination with fire to gain advantage over the enemy.[2] It conjures visions of a base of fire that keeps the enemy's head down while a maneuver element moves around the enemy's flank to assault from behind. Most of us recognize this maneuver as an envelopment.

An envelopment represents one general type of maneuver: **maneuver in space**. We can identify at least one other general type as well: **maneuver in time**. We can perhaps see each of these best by looking at air-to-air combat.

Classic air-to-air combat, as in a World War I dogfight, illustrates maneuver in space. Through turns, climbs, dives, and other moves, each aircraft seeks to gain an advantage in position—usually trying to get behind the enemy, in his six o'clock. Aircraft that can make tighter turns or climb faster or pull out of a dive better than their opponents have an advantage because they can better maneuver in space to get into an advantageous position.

Maneuver in time is shown in air-to-air combat by varying speed or use of energy. Here, in addition to classic dogfight moves, the pilot also varies the speed of his aircraft, trying to combine turns, climbs, and dives with acceleration and deceleration. The pilot wants to run his opponent out of energy—to lead him into going slow at a moment when he will need speed. While the opponent needs to accelerate, which takes time, the pilot uses that time to get into an advantageous position to shoot him down.

We see the same tactics in ground warfare. As noted, an envelopment is maneuver in space; you come around the enemy's flank. When we operate at a faster tempo than the enemy, e.g., if we can attack into his depth faster than he can shift reserves laterally to block us, we maneuver in time. Each type of maneuver gives us leverage; when we can combine them, we get still more leverage.

BUILDING ON ADVANTAGE

Once you have used one or another of these tools to create a decisive advantage and gain leverage, you must exploit it. FMFM 1 emphasizes exploiting opportunities to "create in increasing numbers more opportunities for exploitation."[3] In tactics, you exploit by seizing and maintaining the initiative to create decisive advantages faster than the enemy can cope with them. That means you must think ahead to your next move and the one beyond it: How are you going to use this decisive advantage to create yet another one? For example, in an attack by infiltration, once you have created one decisive advantage by bypassing the enemy's strength and getting into his rear, you create another by pouring forces through the gap you have found or created, generating the "expanding torrent" Liddell-Hart wrote about.[4]

Rommel recounts in *Attacks* how during World War I exploiting each advantage in the battle for Kuk in the

Carpathian mountains led to yet another opportunity. As his detachment exploited each opportunity and moved farther behind the enemy's lines, it generated more surprise and consequent leverage. It was during this action that Rommel's detachment captured thousands of enemy soldiers with very little fighting, due largely to his unwillingness to lose momentum. One success led directly to another opportunity which he immediately seized.[5]

Summary

As we said, leverage is about fighting smart. It is about using judo against an opponent who thinks he is in a fistfight. It is about overrunning his position with infantry as he prepares his antiarmor defenses. It is about not letting him know you are at his six o'clock with your F-18 until your cannon shells are ripping off his wing. It is about doing an impossible maneuver because you have cut loose from your supply line, knowing your logisticians can take another route and meet you before you run out of supplies.

We often see Marines fight this way in field exercises. Often, their role is that of the opposition forces. They fight smart because they are greatly outnumbered. They are generally effective far beyond their numbers because they fight smart. They infiltrate your lines. They capture your command post. They interdict your supply. They ambush you. In short, they fight only when they have a decisive advantage.

The lesson is: to fight smart, gain leverage. However, to be effective, tactics must go beyond merely gaining the upper hand.

Chapter 3

Trapping the Enemy

"In war the power to use two fists is an inestimable asset. To feint with one fist and strike with the other yields an advantage, but still greater advantage lies in being able to interchange them — to convert the feint into the real blow if the opponent uncovers himself."[1]

FMFM 1-3 — Trapping the Enemy

If you read a history of, say, the Civil War, you may get the impression that most battles are glorified shoving matches. One side, the attacker, seeks to push the enemy off a piece of ground. If the attacker succeeds, the defender tries to push him back out again.

World War I often looked like this. After the initial battles, the Allies and the Germans secured their flanks on the English Channel and the Swiss border, creating a continuous front. For nearly three years, attacks consisted of one of these armies rushing across no man's land under murderous fires, attempting to push the opponent out of his earthworks. If the attack proved successful (and few did), the evicted forces would counterattack the same way, attempting to regain their lost terrain. These deadly shoving matches produced no decisive results. The war merely dragged on. The Korean War by 1952, long after the brilliance of Inchon, evolved into much the same thing with forces retaking the same ground time and again, producing only casualties.

The frustration with this kind of carnage was well expressed by F. Scott Fitzgerald's character in *Tender Is the Night*, who revisited the Somme years after the war. "See that little stream—we could walk to it . . . a whole empire walking very slowly, dying in front and pushing forward behind. And another empire walked very slowly backward a few inches a day, leaving the dead like a million bloody rugs."[2]

Tactics ——————————————————— FMFM 1-3

A NEW ORDER

Modern tactics is different. It is based not on pushing the enemy, but on trapping him. In early 1917, the Germans realized that they could not hope to sustain the staggering casualties of trench warfare much longer. They would run out of soldiers long before the Allied powers did. Their solution to this problem was to employ a defense in depth, consisting of many strong points rather than lines, all supported by a strong counterattack force. The idea was to allow the Allies to deeply penetrate and then cut off the penetrating forces. This trapping tactic proved very successful. It allowed the Germans to fight through 1917 and into late 1918.[3]

Why do we want to trap the enemy instead of just push him? Because a pushing contest is seldom decisive. The side that is pushed out comes back the next day, still full of fight. You have to fight him again and again and again. In Vietnam, most of our battles were pushing battles. We were always able to push the enemy off the ground he held and to inflict casualties on him. However, he just withdrew to regroup, replaced his losses, and came back to fight us again. The result was an endless war.

However, if you can trap your enemy, you can win decisively. One prime example from Vietnam of trapping the enemy is Operation Dewey Canyon.

FMFM 1-3 ——————— Trapping the Enemy

During early January 1969, North Vietnamese activity along the Laotian-South Vietnamese border increased dramatically. Large convoys, including armored vehicles, regularly traveled from Laos into South Vietnam. Colonel Robert H. Barrow and his 9th Marines responded with Operation Dewey Canyon.

The three battalions of the regiment crossed the Da Krong River on February 11th and 12th. The Third and First Battalions moved south-southeast through the mountainous terrain toward Laos. Second Battalion, to the west, swung south-southwest, turning east astride the Vietnam-Laos border. The North Vietnamese forces moving along Route 922 from Laos into the A Shau Valley were trapped between the three battalions. They were mauled. For every Marine killed, the North Vietnamese lost a dozen. Their equipment losses were staggering. More importantly, Dewey Canyon destroyed a North Vietnamese base area and disrupted their logistics to the point of pre-empting their spring offensive in I Corps.[4]

Battles like this <u>are</u> decisive. The enemy force engaged is gone, vanished; it cannot return to fight you again. Most of history's decisive battles have been trapping actions, from Marathon to Stalingrad. Therefore, your goal in tactics is always to put the enemy in a trap. What are some ways you can do this?

Pincers

One way is to trap the enemy in pincers. You are familiar with pincers in the form of a nutcracker. Alone, each arm of the nutcracker can only push, but when the two arms are joined, they become a trap. The nut, which is damaged not at all by being pushed around, is crushed between the arms of a nutcracker.

Consider the case of an enemy rifleman shooting at you from behind a tree. If you fire at him only from the front, he is protected by the tree. If you go around him and start firing from his rear, he can simply go to the other side of the tree and still have the same degree of protection. However, if there are two of you and one fires at the enemy rifleman from the front while the other fires at him from the rear, you have put him in a pincer. If he faces toward the front, he exposes his unprotected back. If he faces toward the rear, he exposes his back to your buddy. He remains vulnerable no matter what he does. The arms of the nutcracker, equal in strength, have him.

Good tactics work like a nutcracker. They crush the enemy between two or more different actions that become your pincers. For example, you can use fire and movement; the fire causes the enemy to seek cover, but while covered he cannot respond effectively to your movement. Or, you can

FMFM 1-3 — Trapping the Enemy

put pressure on the enemy's front while attacking into one or both of his flanks; he cannot respond to all your actions at once. You may seek to cut off your enemy and encircle him; this adds psychological to physical pressure. Many of history's decisive battles illustrate some form of pincer tactics. Leuctra is a good example.

In 371 B.C., two opposing Greek forces assembled near the city of Thebes at Leuctra. Ten thousand Spartans under King Cleombrotus I were organized into a phalanx — a mass of troops eight ranks deep. In phalanx tactics, two phalanxes advanced on and collided with one another. Usually, not much happened; battles were normally indecisive.

At the opposite end of the field, 6,000 Thebans under Epaminondas prepared for battle. Greatly outnumbered, Epaminondas realized the futility of throwing his small force against the Spartan phalanx. Contrary to the rules of his day, Epaminondas organized his forces unevenly, placing the bulk of his heavy infantry on his left, 48 ranks deep. His remaining forces formed thin ranks to his right and center. These were echeloned to his right rear.

Epaminondas initiated the attack by immediately charging with his weighted left while his center and right advanced slowly. Aside from being hopelessly confused by this original tactic, the eight-rank Spartan phalanx could not withstand the massed Theban attack on their right. The Spartan right collapsed. Epaminondas then wheeled against the exposed Spartan flank just as his center and right joined the battle. Facing Thebans on their flank and front (a pincer), the Spartans fled, leaving 2,000 dead on the field.

A good modern small-unit example comes from the experience of a French company in the opening days of World War I. As the Frenchmen moved up a small draw, groups of German riflemen infiltrated among the trees above them on either side. The Germans formed a horseshoe around the advancing Frenchmen and opened fire. The French lieutenant forced his men into a skirmish line and attacked into the ambushers; however, the farther they advanced, the more they exposed themselves to German crossfire. Although the French soldiers bravely returned fire, the crossfire proved overwhelming and their ranks broke. The attack became a rout. In this case, the fire from two directions provided the pincers, the arms of the nutcracker.[5]

Pincer tactics also play in aviation. It is a common technique in air-to-air combat. Upon detecting enemy aircraft, a flight of fighters splits into two or more elements beyond air-to-air missile range. The idea is to approach the enemy aircraft from as many directions as possible, not only from the flanks but at varying altitudes. No matter how he moves—dives, climbs, turns, or twists in a combination of moves—he is exposed.

The pincer is one way of trapping the enemy, but the nutcracker concept can be carried further. It has been one of the central concepts of modern tactics: combined arms.

COMBINED ARMS

Modern tactics are combined arms tactics; on that, virtually every modern military is in agreement. What is meant by combined arms?

The Marine Corps is the only truly integrated air-ground-logistic team in the world. The MAGTF is often called a combined arms team. From the Marine Corps' standpoint, a combined arms team means one that has all the elements necessary for sustained combat and noncombat operations: combat, combat support, and combat service support. Combined arms in this context means combining all these assets to fight on the battlefield.

There is, however, another definition of combined arms which is fundamental to maneuver warfare. It is the idea of posing the enemy not just with a problem, but with a *dilemma*—a no-win situation. You combine your supporting arms, organic fires, and maneuver in such a way that the action which the enemy takes to avoid one threat makes him more vulnerable to another.[6]

Suppose an enemy fired at you from a fighting hole. Firing at him from two directions might force him to take cover in the bottom of his hole where he would be safe. If, however, you drove him to ground with rifle fire and then dropped a hand grenade in the hole, you face him with a dilemma. He can either get out of his hole, run for safer lodgings, and face the rifle fire; or he can stay in his hole and face the grenade. Either way, he loses. That is what combined arms is all about: giving the enemy equally distasteful choices and trapping him "between a rock and a hard place."

An enemy mechanized column suddenly encounters a hasty minefield. If the enemy commander tries to run through the minefield, he will undoubtedly lose vehicles and men. If he dismounts his infantry to move them around it while the drivers traverse it with empty vehicles, we call in airburst artillery fire. If he waits too long to decide, our on-call aircraft and direct support artillery attack the column. That is combined arms.

FMFM 1-3 ——————————— **Trapping the Enemy**

SURPRISE

In tactics, not all trapping is based on pincers. If you think about trapping a mouse in your house, you will quickly see another way to trap an enemy: *surprise*. The mousetrap springs and catches the mouse before it can react to save itself. In military tactics, we do the same thing with an ambush. We pounce upon him with concentrated fires, devastating him before he can react. As discussed earlier, an ambush depends on surprise.

Again, as with pincers, the use of surprise runs all through tactics. Since air-to-air combat began in 1915, between 60 and 80 percent of all planes destroyed in air-to-air combat were shot down by someone they never saw.

Surprise is also possible in logistics. How? On more than one occasion, one side in a conflict launched an unexpected offensive based on a logistics surprise. Their opponent had calculated that an attack was impossible for logistics reasons; the enemy simply could not have enough supplies to launch an attack because its supply lines were being bombed or otherwise attacked or because of the weather or terrain. Nevertheless, the attacker had, with great secrecy, built up sufficient supplies. Its logisticians surprised the enemy.

One such instance of logistical surprise was at Dien Bien Phu, a French outpost in northwest Vietnam. Contrary to French expectations, the Viet Minh moved hundreds of artillery pieces into the surrounding mountains. The Vietnamese did the impossible by dismantling the field pieces and man-packing them through the jungle and up the mountains. The French were caught unawares. The Vietnamese quickly put all the French artillery out of commission and eventually overran the French garrison.

Whether used in ground combat, air combat, or logistical preparation for combat, traps often depend on surprise. Surprise takes the enemy unawares. This raises the question, How do you take the enemy unawares?

Uncertainty and deception

There are two basic answers: uncertainty and deception. Both are central elements in modern tactics because both are central to the art of trapping the enemy.

Uncertainty is a central characteristic of war. FMFM 1, *Warfighting*, says of it:

> All actions in war take place in an atmosphere of uncertainty—the fog of war. Uncertainty pervades

battle in the form of unknowns about the enemy, about the environment, and even about the friendly situation.[7]

In tactics, the challenge is to use this uncertainty to trap the enemy.

A common way to use uncertainty in tactics is to lead the enemy to try to cover all the bases because he is uncertain where your attack will come. The result is that he is weak everywhere—including where you actually attack. Insurgent or hit-and-run tactics are a good example of this. By striking hard but randomly, a relatively small force can often tie up a much larger force. Such was the case with Confederate Colonel John Mosby and his raiders. By remaining amorphous and unpredictable, Mosby's raiders kept several divisions of Union troops out of battle.

Sometimes, you can generate useful uncertainty through secrecy. More often you create it through ambiguity. It is usually difficult to conceal all your movements from your enemy, but you can confuse him as to the meaning of what he sees. That, in turn, sets him up to be surprised. A good example was Iraq's invasion of Kuwait in August 1990. The Iraqi build-up along the border adjacent to Kuwait was observed and widely reported. Through diplomacy, the Iraqis kept its meaning ambiguous. Most observers thought it was intended to put pressure on Kuwait to yield in negotiations that were then taking place. When Iraq actually invaded, it achieved virtually total surprise. Kuwait's army was trapped in its garrisons.

Ambiguity was central to the tactics of the World War II German *blitzkrieg*. An attack in *blitzkrieg* involved multiple thrusts with reinforcements following whichever thrusts were most successful. The multitude of thrusts created paralyzing uncertainty in the opponent because he could not determine which constituted the real attack. (Of course, with flexible reinforcement of success, all of them were potentially real.) There was nothing secret about the German attack, but it was ambiguous on a massive scale.

Sometimes, secrecy or (more commonly) ambiguity goes beyond creating uncertainty and results in deception. A deceived enemy is not uncertain; he is certain, but wrong. The German attack on France in 1940 is a good example. The French were certain the main German attack would come through Holland and northern Belgium. When instead the Germans made their main effort through the Ardennes, the French could not react effectively. They had been certain, but wrong.[8]

In 1973, the Israelis were similarly deceived by the Egyptians who used ambiguity to generate deception. The

Egyptians had repeatedly maneuvered in ways that suggested an attack. Egypt's President Anwar Sadat said over and over that he would attack and did not, to the point where it became something of a joke. When finally the Egyptians really meant it, the Israelis dismissed the warning signs as yet another maneuver or bluff. They were certain Egypt would not attack. They were wrong.[9]

SUMMARY

Pincers, surprise, uncertainty, deception, integration of all assets to create combined arms — all have the same purpose in tactics: *trapping the enemy in such a way that he has no escape*. That is how you fight and win decisive engagements and battles. The success of Operation Desert Storm attests to the effectiveness of these principles. Just pushing the enemy around usually accomplishes little, and pushing tactics rightly belong largely to history. Marine Corps tactics — maneuver tactics — demand more than that. They demand that Marines, in every fight, strive to achieve a decision. Almost always, that means catching the enemy in some kind of trap.

Chapter 4

Moving Faster

"Open warfare demands elastic tactics, quick decisions, and swift maneuvers. Mobility includes far more than mere rapidity of movement. From the leader it demands prompt dicisions, clear, concise orders, anticipation of the probable course of action and some sure means for the rapid transmission of orders. From the troops it demands promptness in getting started, the ability to make long marches under the most adverse conditions of terrain and weather, skill in effecting rapid deployments and abrupt changes of formation without delay or confusion, facility in passing from the defensive to the offensive, or the reserve, and finally, a high morale. In brief, then, mobility implies both rapidity and flexibility."[1]

FMFM 1-3 — Moving Faster

Usually, when you think of your weapons, you think of your personal M-16 or pistol, your unit's machine guns, mortars, and AT-4s, or your aircraft's Sidewinders or bombs or rockets. If you are a logistician, you may realize your weapons are also your trucks. Some Marines overlook one of their most powerful weapons, a weapon that serves infantrymen, aviators, and logisticians equally. That weapon is speed.

SPEED IN COMBAT

How is speed a weapon? Think of sports: The breakaway in hockey uses speed as a weapon. By rapidly passing the puck down the ice, one team denies the other the chance to set up a defense. Speed circumvents their opponent's ability to respond in an organized manner. The fastbreak in basketball seeks the same result. In two or three passes, the ball is downcourt, the basket scored, and the team quickly reorganized for the defense, all before the opposition knows what is happening.

The results of speed often reach beyond the immediate goal. How many times have you seen a team score on a fastbreak, steal the ball as it comes inbounds, and immediately score again, and even a third time? Unable to regain their composure, the victims of the fastbreak become the victims of a rally. The rallying team again fastbreaks and scores yet again. The victims lose confidence. Passes go astray; signals become crossed; tempers flare; arguments ensue. The rally becomes a rout. The beleaguered players see certain defeat. They virtually give up while still on the field of play.

The same thing happens in combat. The battalion or fighter aircraft or logistics train that can consistently *move and act* faster than its enemy has a tremendous advantage.

In 1862, Stonewall Jackson moved his foot cavalry up and down the Shenandoah Valley against several larger Union forces. His corps' ability to quickly move considerable distances, strike, delay, move, and strike again tied up three times his numbers in Union forces. His speed in movement and action convinced Union leaders that a significant Confederate invasion force stood ready to attack Washington, D.C. As a result, Jackson's actions denied reinforcements to the Union General McClellan in his peninsula campaign. Jackson's speed offered immense advantage with relatively little risk to his limited manpower.

The British aviators bested the Germans during the Battle of Britain of World War II in part because they could reconstitute and redistribute fighter squadrons faster than the Germans could sortie. After each German bombing raid, the British quickly assessed their casualties and transferred combat-effective units into the active areas. The ineffective squadrons rotated out of action to recover and refit. Thus, German fighter and bomber pilots constantly faced fresh British pilots in serviceable airplanes. Eventually, German aircraft and pilot losses forced the Germans to end daylight bombing and resort strictly to night bombing sorties.

The great captains repeatedly commented on the value of speed in combat. Napoleon said, "I may lose a battle, but I will never lose a minute."[2] Nathan Bedford Forrest told the secret of his many victories: " . . . get there first with the most men."[3] General Heinz Guderian's nickname was *schneller* Heinz—fast Heinz. General Hermann Balck's motto for his staff was, "Don't work hard—work fast!"[4] History's great captains differed in many ways, but one thing they shared was a sense of the importance of speed.

In Operation Urgent Fury in 1983, Battalion Landing Team 2/8, under Lieutenant Colonel Ray Smith, moved fast, as he had trained them to do. When they captured the operations officer of the Grenadian army, he said to them, "You appeared so swiftly in so many places where we didn't expect you that it was clear that resistance was hopeless, so I recommended to my superiors that we lay down our arms and go into hiding."[5] That is what speed used as a weapon can do for you.

WHAT IS SPEED?

This question would seem to have a simple answer: Speed is going fast. It is speed as we think of it when driving a car — more miles per hour.

That is part of the answer in tactics as well. For example, when a Soviet tank battalion attacks, it goes over the ground as fast as it can — at as many meters per minute as it can. General Balck was asked whether the Russian tanks ever used terrain in their attacks against him in World War II. He replied that they had used terrain on occasion, but that they usually used speed. The questioner followed up: "Which was harder to defend against?" Balck answered, "Speed."[6]

Physical speed, more meters per minute or miles per hour, is a powerful weapon in itself. On your approach to the enemy, speed narrows his reaction time. When you are going through him or around him, it changes his situation faster than he can react. Once you are past him, it makes his reaction irrelevant. In all three cases, speed gets inside his mind, causing fear, indecision, helplessness.

Speed and Time

There is more to speed in a military sense than simply going fast. First, there is a sense of *time*, and there is also a sense of *timing*. Speed and time are closely related. In fact, speed is defined in terms of time: miles or kilometers per hour. In tactics, what this means is that time is always of the utmost importance.

Even when you are engaged with the enemy, you are not always moving fast. Some of the time, you are not moving at all. Nonetheless, every moment is still of the utmost importance even when you are sitting still. A brigade staff that takes a day to plan an action is slower than one that takes an hour. A tank battalion that takes three hours to refuel is slower than one that takes two hours, just as one that must refuel every hundred miles is slower than one that must refuel every two hundred. A company that sits down to eat once it has taken its objective is slower than one that immediately presses on into the enemy's depth. A fighter squadron that can fly only three sorties per aircraft per day is slower, in terms of effect on the enemy, than one that flies six. A maintenance repair team that takes two days to fix a damaged vehicle and get it back into action is slower, in terms of effect on the enemy, than one that can do it overnight.

Making maximum use of every hour and every minute is as important to speed in combat as simply going fast when you are moving. It is important to every member of a military force whether serving on staffs or in units—aviation, resupply and repair, ground combat, everything. A good tactician has within him a constant sense of urgency. He feels guilty if he is idle. He never wastes time, and he is never content with the pace at which events are happening. Like Guderian, he is always saying to himself and to others, "Faster! Faster!" He knows that if speed is a weapon, so is time.

Timing

Time, and the need to make maximum use of it, is also related to timing. At first glance, the two may seem to be in contention. Maximizing the use of time would appear to require acting at the earliest opportunity. On the contrary, timing may require *deliberate delay*. For example, if you are on the defensive, you may want to let an enemy penetration develop itself so that your counterattack, when it comes, bags the largest possible enemy force. One of the most common errors when on the defensive is counterattacking too soon so that the enemy is merely pushed back rather than cut off, encircled, and destroyed. Timing, in other words, seems to require that you sometimes sacrifice speed by waiting.

Generally, the contradiction is more apparent than real. The reason is that the results of your timing—a greater defeat for the enemy—give you the opportunity for greater speed over the longer run. The most frequent source of delay is the enemy. The greater the defeat you inflict on him in one situation, the less he will be able to delay you subsequently. So timing, instead of being in tension with time and in conflict with a sense of urgency, is actually a more skillful use of time.

RELATIVE SPEED

Going fast and making maximum use of time are both parts of the answer to the question, "What is speed?" However, there remains something else to be considered: the enemy. As with all things in war, speed is relative. *It is only meaningful militarily if you are acting faster than the enemy.* You can do that either by slowing the enemy or by hastening yourself.

In the battle for the Falkland Islands in 1982, the British Army moved slowly. The terrain was difficult, the weather was abominable, and much of the material had to be moved on men's backs, all of which slowed down the British. Nevertheless, the British still had the advantage in speed, because they moved faster than the Argentines who, once they had made their initial dispositions, essentially did not move at all. That superiority in relative speed gave the British the initiative throughout the campaign.

Continuous Speed

To be decisive, a *superiority in relative speed must be constant*. It is not enough to move faster than the enemy only now and then because when we are not moving faster, the advantage, the initiative, passes to him. This need to operate continually faster makes the challenge more difficult. Most forces can manage a burst of speed now and then, provided they can then halt for a considerable period to recover. During that halt, they are likely to lose the advantage in speed over time . . . the consistent advantage.

Here the speediness of the logistics or combat service support element of the MAGTF becomes of critical importance. Although physical exhaustion is often a factor, halts usually are driven by logistics: ground or aviation units must stop to catch up on maintenance and supplies. Nonetheless, supporting forces can minimize loss of speed if they can move and operate fast. If they can deliver the supplies and perform the maintenance quickly, the combat units can move again before the enemy gains the initiative.

Speed and Change

In order to act consistently faster than the enemy, it is necessary to do more than move fast in whatever you are doing.

FMFM 1-3 — Moving Faster

It is also necessary to make *rapid transitions* from one action to another. In the 18th century, the importance of fast transitions (sometimes called agility) was often seen in the need to shift from column formation into line. If an army was caught by an enemy while still in column and could not rapidly deploy in line, it was often beaten. Much drill practice was devoted to making this difficult transition so that it could be accomplished rapidly in combat. A modern example of the importance of fast transitions comes from aerial combat.

In the Korean War, American aviators achieved a high kill ratio of about 10:1 over their North Korean and Chinese opponents. At first glance, this is somewhat surprising. The main enemy fighter, the MiG-15, was superior to the American F-86 in a number of key respects. It could climb and accelerate faster, and it had a better sustained turn rate. The F-86, however, was superior to the MiG in two critical, though less obvious, respects. First, because it had high-powered hydraulic controls, the F-86 could shift from one maneuver to another faster than the MiG. Second, because of its bubble canopy, the F-86 pilot had better visibility. The F-86's better field of vision also contributed to fast transitions because it allowed its pilot to understand changing situations more quickly.

American pilots developed new tactics based on these dual superiorities. When they engaged the MiGs, they sought to put them through a series of changing maneuvers. At each change, the F-86's faster transitions gave it a time advantage which the pilot transformed into a position advantage. Often, when the MiG pilots realized what was happening, they panicked — and thereby made the American pilot's job all the easier.

These tactics illustrate the way fast transitions relate to overall speed and to time. They also show the importance of time and speed in a broader sense which has been brought out in the work of Colonel John Boyd, USAF (Ret). Colonel Boyd studied a wide variety of historic battles, campaigns, and wars. He noted that where numerically inferior forces had defeated their opponents, they often did so by presenting the other side with a sudden, unexpected change or a series of changes. The superior forces fell victim because they could not adjust to the changes in a timely manner. Generally, the defeat came at relatively small cost to the victor.[7]

This research led to the Boyd theory which states that conflict may be viewed as time-competitive cycles of observation-orientation-decision-action. First, each party to a conflict enters the fray by observing himself, his surroundings, his enemy. Second, based upon his observations, he orients to the situation, that is, he produces a mental image of his situation. Next, based upon this orientation, he makes a decision. Last, he puts the decision into effect — he acts. On the assumption that his action has changed the situation, he again observes, beginning the cycle anew. Actions continue to follow Boyd's cycle, often called an OODA (observation, orientation, decision, action) loop.

The Boyd theory defines the word "maneuver" in the term "maneuver warfare." It means being consistently faster than your opponent. As your enemy observes and orients on your action, you must be observing, orienting, deciding, and acting upon your second action. As you enact your third, fourth, and fifth move, your enemy falls behind in a panicked game of catch up. The time gap between your actions and his reactions increasingly widens. As he tries to respond to your penetration, you attack his reserves and his command and control. As he counterattacks with his mobile reserve, you by-pass with helicopterborne forces. Everything he does is too late.

Colonel Boyd's research showed that historically forces faced with these continuous changes panicked or became passive. In the first case, they generally retreated. In the second, they surrendered. In either case, victory resulted from speed.

Thus, you see that the military answer to the question "What is speed?" is not simple. Nonetheless, it is central to every aspect of tactics, especially in the context of maneuver warfare doctrine. As General George Patton said, "In small operations, as in large, speed is the essential element of success."[8]

Becoming faster

Now you see clearly the importance of speed in tactics and why it is one of the basic concepts that shape tactics for ground, air, and combat service support. You want to be fast. How do you do it?

You start by having a sense of the importance of time. We already noted this, but mention it again here because many of us must make a change.

We, as Marines and leaders of Marines, have a responsibility to make things happen fast. If some set process gets in the way of operating fast, change it or get rid of it. You are responsible for results, not method. Your sense of the importance of time, of urgency, must direct your actions. You must work to create and build that sense within yourself.

Once you have it, there are a number of things you can do to increase speed. First, you can *keep <u>everything</u> simple*. Simplicity promotes speed; complexity slows things down. Simplicity should be central to your plans, your staffs (large staffs are one of war's greatest consumers of time), your command and control, and to your own actions. Fast decisions on your part, in place of lengthy councils of war, are an important element in simplicity and thus speed.

Second, you go fast by *using mission orders*. Mission orders allow everyone to harmonize efforts by knowing what result they are collectively attempting to achieve. Each person can act quickly as the situation changes without having to delay to pass information up the chain of command and wait for orders to come back down.

By 1815, the Prussian Army was already well advanced in the use of mission orders. General Friedrich Müffling detailed as the Prussian liaison officer to Wellington's army, was with the British at Waterloo. There, at one point, Müffling saw Napoleon's Imperial Guard halt. He sensed this as a critical moment in the battle and urged two British brigade commanders to attack with their cavalry. Both commanders agreed on the excellence of the opportunity. However, both refused to take action because they had not received orders to do so.[9] Without orders from Wellington, they could not act. General Müffling was astounded, but the British commanders expressed no misgivings. Throughout the 19th century and well into the 20th, the British Army remained noted for the slowness of most of its actions, while the Prussians had precisely the opposite reputation.

Third, you can *rely heavily on implicit communications.* Implicit communications are mutual understandings that require little or no actual talking. The commanding officer of Charlie Company on your left flank is well-known to you. You think alike because your battalion commander has established SOPs and has schooled his officers in his approach to war. Thus, you do not need to talk with the Charlie Company commander very often in action because you know how he is likely to react to many different situations. If you create an opportunity for him, you know he will take advantage of it. That is implicit communication. It is faster and more reliable than explicit communication (trying to pass words or messages back and forth over radios or other equipment).

Of course, if you intend to raise your speed by using implicit communications, that implies that you take some other actions. It implies keeping people together in their units and stable in their assignments. It implies keeping good teams together. It implies developing a band of brothers in your unit, as Admiral Horatio Nelson did. He spent many evenings with his captains gathered in the cabin of his flagship talking over tactics, ways they might fight different engagements, how they would defeat this or that opponent. From those evenings came a shared way of thinking so strong that, at Trafalgar, Nelson needed only to signal "England expects every man will do his duty," and "close action."[10] They needed no more instruction than that.

Fourth, speed is greatly increased by decentralization. Mission orders are key to decentralization, as you know. Another key is *lateral communication*. If all communication is up and down the chain of command, action will move slowly. But if commanders and leaders at every level communicate laterally—if you, as a leader, talk directly to other leaders—action moves much faster. Lateral communication is in fact a natural consequence of mission orders. It represents a letting go on the part of the higher commander that follows after he states his intent and gives his subordinates their missions.

A good example of lateral communication comes from aviation. In the air, a squadron of aircraft communicates laterally as a matter of course. If one pilot needs to talk to another, he does so. He does not go through the mission commander and then wait for him to talk to the other pilot. Events would quickly outpace communication if he did. The same should be true of ground combat and logistics units as well.

Fifth, you can speed things up by *putting the commander forward*, at the anticipated focus of effort. If he is in the rear, trying to command with maps and telephones, events will often move faster than he can. If he is forward, at the focus of effort, he can instantly make the adjustments necessary as the situation develops.

Throughout World War I and while in command of 7th Panzer Division in France during May through June of 1941, Erwin Rommel led his formations from the front. He achieved extraordinary success during both wars almost entirely as a result of this style of command. Even as a corps and later an army commander, Rommel led from the front. During his defeat of the British field army in Libya and the seizure of Tobruk, he accompanied the advanced elements of the combat forces which he sensed were at the crucial point in the battle. Amid the climate of danger, uncertainty, and confusion, Rommel reduced friction and grasped fleeting opportunities through his personal, physical presence with the forward elements of attacking forces.[11]

Sixth, *improvisation* is of critical importance to raising speed. Often, you will find yourself in a situation where your assets — weapons, vehicles, etc. — are not adequate to keep you moving fast. Some of them may even be hindrances in your particular situation. When that happens, improvise. If you don't have enough mines, make some. If you do not have enough vehicles to move all your men, get some from the local economy. In France in 1940, Guderian put some of his infantry in commandeered French buses. On Grenada, when Army Rangers needed vehicles, they took East German trucks belonging to the Grenadian army. Sound extreme? If the situation were not extreme, you would not be improvising!

War—successful war—is filled with improvisation. You should start to learn how to improvise now, in your training. Leaders should value this innovative thinking. Moreover, they should expect it from their subordinates because it offers new opportunities.

For improvisation to be effective, commanders must readily exploit the opportunities uncovered by subordinates. Commanders cannot remain tied to plans that blind them to fleeting opportunities. While making the best possible preparations, they must welcome the unforeseen.

Finally, *experience* breeds speed. This is why veteran units are usually much faster than green, untried units. If you are familiar with a situation, or at least know generally what to expect, you can think, act, and move faster. In peacetime, your Marines are not likely to be veterans. Still, you can give them experience through tactical decision games, sand table exercises, war games, and field exercises.

SUMMARY

You may think of additional ways to be fast. That is to the good. When you find one that works, tell your fellow Marines about it so they can use it too. Anything that works to make you faster is good whether or not it is in the books.

Chapter 5

Cooperating

"Unity of effort is coordinated action toward a common goal; it is cooperation. It is the working together by all commanders toward the accomplishment of a common mission, which is imperative for complete and final success. Commanders must develop in their staffs and subordinates the desire to cooperate, not only among themselves but with other elements . . ."[1]

Each of these principles of tactics—gaining a decisive advantage, moving faster than the enemy, trapping the enemy, and the goal of all of them, achieving a decisive result—presents something of a dilemma. Each requires different elements, different units, and different Marines to work effectively together. If efforts are not in harmony, results will be indecisive. If, for example, the actions of aviation are not integrated with the ground battle, they are unlikely to have a decisive effect. If artillery support is not well coordinated with an infantry attack, you will not have the force of combined arms, and the attack will likely fail.

Control in Combat?

At the same time, because war is characterized by disorder, uncertainty, and rapid change, control in combat quickly breaks down. It is probably a mistake to speak of *control* in combat. As anyone who has survived combat will undoubtedly testify, it is one of the hardest of all human endeavors to control. In fact, it is impossible to control if by that we mean one man carefully directing the actions of others.

The dilemma is sharpened by the fact that attempts to control men in combat easily undermine initiative. You are not likely to trap, or move faster, or gain leverage over a competent opponent without a great deal of initiative from

Marines at every level, down through private. Yet efforts to control those Marines too often work against initiative, by teaching them not to act without orders. That kind of control undermines the initiative upon which our tactics depend.

The dilemma, then, is this: How do we achieve the goal of working together in harmony without some sort of centralized control?

COOPERATION

The beginning of an answer lies in the word *cooperation*. Cooperation, rightly understood, is the opposite of control. Control works top down: someone up above determines what you will and what you will not do and makes you conform to his dictates. Cooperation, in contrast, works laterally and also bottom up. You take the initiative to help those around you accomplish your shared mission.

Cooperation is essential to modern tactics. The flight leader and wingman work on the basis of cooperation; the Cobra pilots and the infantry they support cooperate; two infantry units, fighting side by side, cooperate; a mobile combat service support detachment and a mechanized force cooperate. We all work together far more effectively when we communicate laterally than when we talk only through a higher headquarters and respond only to centralized direction.

The history of tactics is rife with examples where cooperation made the difference — and control could not have done so. One such involves the reconnaissance battalion of a German armored division during operations east of the Russian city of Kharkov on September 3, 1942.

For several hours, Major Kurt Meyer had moved his battalion along a narrow trail in deep snow through heavily wooded terrain in hope of interdicting the main road north of Kharkov. Progress was very slow. Only the fact that he could not turn his vehicles and tanks around in the close terrain kept him moving forward.

As his main body entered a clearing, Major Meyer noticed that his vanguard company had left the trail to conceal themselves in the trees on the far side of the clearing. Halting the column, Meyer crawled forward. From the trees on the far side of the clearing, the terrain sloped down to a road and rose again on the other side of it. To his astonishment, the road held several thousand Russians moving west toward Belgorod, recently occupied by German forces. These were fresh troops, supported by vehicles, artillery, and tanks. Overwhelmingly outnumbered and outgunned, Meyer ordered his battalion to move off the trail and into the woods and to remain quiet, hoping to avoid detection.

About to conceal themselves, the Germans suddenly heard the drone of aircraft. Halting the battalion, Meyer recognized the aircraft as German Stuka dive-bombers. The bombers, upon seeing the dense column, circled to gain altitude and began bombing and strafing the Russians. Pandemonium followed. Meyer, seizing upon the confusion, immediately ordered his companies to attack. When the Panzers emerged from the trees, the aircraft signaled recognition.

As the Stukas worked up and down the column, Meyer's Panzers blocked the Russians fleeing up his slope toward the trees. The far slope was a barren snowfield that offered no cover. Hundreds of Russians were killed, and hundreds more surrendered. The action prevented an estimated corps-sized unit from attacking the German assembly area at Belgorod.[2]

The example shows what cooperation, unplanned and uncommunicated, can accomplish. The aircraft were unexpected. Meyer's Panzers were present by coincidence. The aircraft had no radios with which to contact the tank unit. The outnumbered Panzers could not have attacked the Russians single-handedly. Undoubtedly, an air strike alone would have damaged the Russian column, but without the immediate cooperation of Meyer's Panzers it would not have been decisive.

FMFM 1-3 ——————————————— Cooperating

DISCIPLINE

Cooperation resolves the dilemma of finding a way to harmonize efforts, to get everyone working together without creating the centralized control that undermines initiative. It also raises another question: How do we get people to cooperate?

The answer is the foundation of effective tactics: *discipline*. Discipline is one of the basic components of tactics. It underlies all the other components because without it, you will not be able to gain leverage, maintain superior relative speed, or trap the enemy—or attain a decision, for that matter, which is the purpose of the other three.

However, the discipline needed for cooperation is different from what some may think of when they consider military discipline. It is not imposed discipline, but self-discipline.

Imposed discipline is the discipline of the Prussian army of Frederick the Great, where the object was to make each soldier fear his NCOs and officers more than he feared the enemy. That kind of discipline is part of control, and, as such, it is not appropriate to modern tactics. It is rigid, paralyzing, and utterly destructive of initiative.

Self-discipline is different. It is a moral force. As FMFM 1 states, war is also fought on the moral level. Here, in the matter of discipline, tactics and the moral level intersect. Self-discipline *morally obligates* every Marine to cooperate with every other Marine to achieve the common goal—in battle, a decision. The obligation is *internal*, in each individual; it is something he feels, powerfully. He is pulled from within to do everything he can to support his fellow Marines.

Imposed discipline is useful, if at all, only in the earliest stages of training. For maneuver warfare to work, every Marine needs a potent self-discipline. Why? Because in maneuver warfare everyone must harmonize his efforts—cooperate—at a very high level of initiative.

We can see self-discipline at work in many cases where we also see effective cooperation. This is most evident in successful athletic teams. Team players constantly take it upon themselves to back up their teammates. In baseball, the first baseman immediately covers the catcher on a play at home plate. The shortstop routinely backs up a ground ball to the third baseman, and the outfielders cover each other on flyballs. In hockey, rarely does only one player rush the goal. In football, offensive linemen don't stand by idly on a pass play if no defensive player faces them. They block the first defender to show himself. This cooperation among teammates cannot be enforced by a coach. It depends upon the self-discipline of the individual players.

While Marines have long been noted for their military discipline, we must focus our thinking on the fact that military discipline is self-discipline. What else can we say about it?

First, we can say that it is a heavy responsibility, because it is a *personal responsibility*. No one can shirk it by blaming someone else. No one else can be at fault when each individual is responsible for his own discipline. A discipline failure—often, a failure to act—is a personal failure. It is automatically the full and sole responsibility of the individual who failed.

Second, as military discipline, it is *absolute*. There is no time off. If, in a given situation, someone else is in charge, that does not in the least absolve others from their responsibility to attain the objective, the common goal. It does not reduce to any degree their responsibility to ensure effective cooperation within the unit and beyond it. All share alike discipline's demand that they do everything in their power to gain a decision. No one can "drop his pack," even for a moment.

In this respect, Marines have an advantage. It has been traditional in our Corps for every Marine always to think of himself as a Marine, on duty or off. We see it whenever off-duty Marines take the initiative to help out at the scene of a traffic accident, or act as leaders in their community or church, or otherwise do more than their share. They do so because of something inward, not because they are being compelled through control. That something is self-discipline, and it is not limited to one aspect of life. It is a mind set, *a way of thinking and behaving.* It runs through everything. It is as much part of garrison life as of combat, of combat service support as of the infantry, of time off as of duty time. It is, ultimately, a way of life.

SUMMARY

Modern tactics depends on cooperation, not control. Cooperation, in turn, depends on self-discipline. As a leader of Marines, you must create a climate in which self-discipline, with the high level of initiative it requires, can flourish.

That climate of demand for and support of self-discipline depends upon you. Words are easy; anyone can give an occasional pep talk on the merits of self-discipline. People judge your actions, not your words, in determining their own actions. If you create a climate where self-discipline is expected, you will get it. There will always be some who are incapable of disciplining themselves. We must recognize those individuals for what they are: people who are unfit to be United States Marines. Those who are fit to be Marines will respond to a climate of self-discipline.

Chapter 6

Making It Happen

"Nine-tenths of tactics are certain and taught in books: but the irrational tenth is like the kingfisher flashing across the pool and that is the test of generals. It can only be ensured by instinct, sharpened by thought practicing the stroke so often that at the crisis it is as natural as a reflex."[1]

FMFM 1-3 ——————————— **Making It Happen**

A Marine leader makes it happen. That means we must apply in practical terms the concepts outlined in this book. Merely reading the book will yield no victories. The question remains, "How do we get beyond reading about these concepts and begin applying them?"

TRAINING

Good tactics depend upon sound technical skills. These are the techniques and procedures which enable us to shoot, move, and communicate. Competence at the technical level is achieved through training, the building of skills through repetition. This is called the science of war.

Training develops familiarity with and confidence in weapons and equipment and the specialized skills essential to survive and function in combat. The ultimate aim of training is speed. Whether Marines compute firing data, rearm and refuel aircraft, repair vehicles, stock or transport supplies, or communicate information, the speed of their actions determines the tempo of the overall force. Training develops the competence which enables this effective speed.

At the small-unit level, training involves developing and refining techniques and procedures such as immediate actions, battle drills, and unit SOPs. These apply to all types of forces whether they are a section of aircraft executing air combat maneuvers, a maintenance contact team repairing a vehicle under fire, an artillery gun team conducting a hip shoot, or a rifle squad breaching a position. We develop and refine these measures so units gain and maintain the speed essential for decisive action.

Staffs, as well as units, must train for speed. Staff training should not focus on set procedures or processes. Rather, a staff should train to support a commander's individual approach to tactics. A staff's procedures should reflect the unique tactical approach of the commander and the abilities of each staff member. Operating in this way, staffs avoid the time-consuming work associated with a rigid, formal staff process. Cohesiveness, which can only be achieved through personnel stability, is the key to fast, efficient staffs. Field Marshal Erwin Rommel emphasized that —

> A commander must accustom his staff to a high tempo from the outset, and continuously keep them up to it. If he once allows himself to be satisfied with norms, or anything less than an all out effort, he gives up the race from the starting post, and will sooner or later be taught a bitter lesson.[2]

Training should also prepare Marines for the uniquely physical nature of combat. Living and caring for themselves in a spartan environment, confronting the natural elements, and experiencing the discomfort of being hungry, thirsty, and tired are as essential in preparing for combat duty as any skills training. The point is not training individuals to be miserable, but to adapt to limited resources and harsh conditions.

Likewise, training should establish the ability to act decisively in any environment. This includes operating during inclement weather and periods of limited visibility. To gain advantage and deliver decisive force at a place and time of our choosing demands that we make rain, snow, fog, and darkness our allies. We can neither simulate, anticipate, nor appreciate the inherent friction which these natural factors produce unless we experience them. History is replete with stories of victory gained by forces who maintained the ability to fight amid this natural adversity. Plentiful also are the histories of those forces who failed for lack of this same ability. Training should provide the confidence, hardiness, individual skills, and small-unit proficiency critical to decisive action.

EDUCATION

Success in combat also depends on our ability to combine all the various tools of combat to meet each unique situation. It requires sound decisions rapidly and resolutely executed. The heart of making sound decisions is conceptualizing the battle which was discussed earlier. This is the art of war. A good tactician develops his judgment to the point of having *coup d'oeil*. He does so through education.

While the battlefield affords the most instructive lessons on decision making, the tactical leader cannot wait for war to begin his education. Like the surgeon, we must be familiar and competent in our profession before entering the operating room. The lives of our men hang in the balance.

Our education in tactics must be focused toward developing three qualities within all tactical leaders. The first is *intuitive skill*, the essence of *coup d'oeil*. The tactician must be readily able to recognize and analyze the critical factors in any situation. The enemy's intentions, the weather, the terrain characteristics, the condition of our own forces, these and many other factors concern us as tacticians.

The second quality is *creative ability*. Tactical leaders must be encouraged to devise and pursue unique approaches to military problems. There exist no rules governing ingenuity. The line separating boldness from foolhardiness is drawn with the ink of practiced judgment.

The third quality is *battlefield judgment*. While Marines must act as members of larger organizations, they must also

FMFM 1-3 — Making It Happen

make individual decisions. All Marines must be able to cut to the heart of a situation, identify its important elements, and make clear, unequivocal decisions. Establishing the intent, the focus of effort, and missions; determining when to shift the focus of effort; deciding when to give and when to refuse battle; recognizing and exploiting opportunity; creating advantage; and maintaining tempo are among the critical elements of our tactical philosophy. Our educational approach should emphasize making decisions which incorporate these elements.

Marine leaders need to learn not only how to make good decisions, but also how to <u>make decisions fast</u>. A good decision taken too late is, in combat, a bad decision. Speed in decision making is a key element in speed overall. The confusion of combat can easily lead commanders to delay making a decision while waiting for perfect information. Marine education must lead commanders at all levels to make timely decisions with whatever information is available. General Patton's remark that "A good plan violently executed *now* is better than a perfect plan next week" reinforces this point.[3]

There exists no single vehicle to develop our decision makers; however, any educational approach should be adaptable to all echelons and to all grades. The environment should be informal and conducive to free thinking; there should be no fear of the consequences of making a wrong decision. The following examples may provide some tools for developing tactical decision making in Marines.

Sand Table and Map Exercises

These exercises present students with a general situation, mission orders from higher headquarters, and minimum information on enemy and friendly forces. Sand table exercises are especially suited to novice tacticians since a sand table presents the terrain in three-dimensional array whereas a map requires interpretation. In both cases, students offer their vision of the battle, deliver their decisions, and issue orders to subordinates. Then those are discussed and criticized. The discussion should emphasize making a decision in the absence of perfect information or complete intelligence. There is no school solution — only sound or unsound judgment based upon reason.

Terrain Walks

Terrain walks introduce the realities of terrain, vegetation, and weather. There are several ways to conduct terrain walks. The desired end results of all are, however, decisions.

The first method provides students with an area of operations, a general and enemy situation usually shown on a map, and a mission. As in sand table and map exercises students derive and support their view of the battle. Choosing one plan, the group then begins to walk the terrain according to the plan. The group not only encounters unanticipated terrain and obstacles, but the instructors introduce enemy actions into the play of the problem. In this way students must confront the uncertainty and disorder which terrain, vegetation, inaccurate maps, and the enemy bring to battle.

The second method involves historical battle studies. When opportunity permits, past battlefields should be traversed with an eye for both sides. Special note should be given to the commanders' decisions. We gain a special vantage on battle by walking the ground and seeing the battlefield from the commanders' perspective. We receive a new appreciation for the blunders of commanders that history has condemned as obvious. The art in decision making quickly becomes evident.

TEWTs

Tactical exercises without troops, or TEWTs, provide tactical leaders opportunities to exercise judgment. The general and enemy situations usually do not change during these exercises. There are two approaches to conducting them.

The first method provides a leader an opportunity to evaluate a subordinate's ability to perform in a given scenario. This method places students in an area of operations and provides a situation upon which to plan and execute a task; e.g., "Establish a reverse slope defense."

The second method also places students in an area of operations and provides a situation, but they are then provided general guidance in the form of a mission order; e.g., "Prevent enemy movement north of Route 348." After walking the ground, the students must first decide whether to defend or attack, supporting their conclusions with reasoning. The reasoning is then discussed and criticized. Preparations for the attack or the defense may follow. This approach encourages the students to put forth maximum ingenuity and initiative. They have free rein to achieve the desired results.

Wargaming

Educating our Marines to think about battle, develop *coup d'oeil*, and acquire practical experience is not limited to map work and countryside jaunts. The playing of war games is essential for all Marines to understand the factors weighing upon the leader's decisions. Morale, the enemy and friendly situations, the higher commander's intentions, firepower, mobility, and terrain are only a few of the decision factors included in the play of war games. In all these simulations, from the sand table to the TACWAR board to the CAS trainer, predictability should be constantly under assault. The less predictable the environment, the more creativity the student must display.

PROFESSIONAL READING AND HISTORICAL STUDY

Critical to developing *coup d'oeil* is the study of military history. Through it, we see how successful commanders thought through the situations facing them. A few people—very few—can do it instinctively. They have what we might call the Nathan Bedford Forrest touch, the inherent ability to think militarily. Most people are not that lucky. We have to work to develop *coup d'oeil*.

In our studies of historical battles, we find the clearest details and most readily available sources of information on our profession. The leadership considerations, the horrors of war, the sacrifices endured, the commitment involved, the resources required, and much more may all be found in a wealth of available books, unit histories, after-action reports, films, and documentaries. Naval, air, and ground battles may all be addressed through this medium. Both individual study and group discussions expand our perspective on the decisions of leaders.

Exercises

While both training and education provide the essential ingredients of combat, tactical success evolves from their synthesis: *the creative application of technical skills based on original, sound judgment.* Exercises enable individuals, units, and staffs to use their skills while leaders at all echelons face decisions in a real-time scenario. Exercises also serve as proving grounds for immediate actions, battle drills, and combat SOPs. Any procedure or technique which does not stand up to the test should be replaced or improved.

An exercise should serve as an internal assessment of the quality of training and education. The conclusions should aim *not to penalize poor performance but to note shortfalls* so as to address them through future instruction. A unit will never be fully trained. There will always be room for improvement.

Exercises also test the ability of units to sustain operating tempo for an extended period of time. Since decisive results are rarely the product of initial actions, the ability to operate and sustain combat effectiveness over time is critical. Exercises should not become 4- or 5- or 10-day waiting games. Knowing when hostilities will cease is a convenience spared the combat soldier. Equipment must be maintained, and people sustained with adequate rest, nourishment, and hygiene until they achieve their mission. The aim is to develop warriors whose only concern is the job ahead. Whenever possible, the duration of exercises should be tied to achieving specific aims.

COMPETITION

Exercises should provide realism. The means to achieve tactical realism is free-play or force-on-force exercises. Whenever possible, unit training should be conducted in a free-play scenario. This approach can be used by all leaders to develop their subordinates. It affords both leaders and unit members the opportunity to apply their skills and knowledge against an active threat.

Free play is adaptable to all tactical scenarios and beneficial to all echelons. Whether it is fire teams scouting against fire teams, sections of aircraft dueling in the sky, or companies, battalions, squadrons and MAGTFs fighting one another, both leaders and individual Marines benefit. Leaders form and execute their decisions against an opposing force as individual Marines employ their skills against an active enemy. Through free play, Marines learn to fight as an organization.

CRITIQUES

A key attribute of decision makers is their ability to justify decisions with *clear reasoning*. Critiques elicit this reasoning process. Any tactical decision game or tactical exercise should culminate with a critique.

The standard approach for conducting critiques should promote initiative. Since every tactical situation is unique, and since no training situation can encompass even a small fraction of the peculiarities of a real tactical situation, there can be no ideal or school solutions. Critiques should focus on the student's rationale for doing what he did. What factors did he consider, or not consider, in making his estimate of the situation? Were the actions taken consistent with this estimate? How well were orders communicated? Were the actions taken tactically sound? Did they have a reasonable chance of being successful? These questions among others should form the basis for critiques. The purpose is to broaden a leader's analytical powers, experience level, and base of knowledge, thereby enhancing his creative ability to devise sound, innovative solutions to difficult problems.

Critiques should be lenient and understanding, rather than bitter and harsh. Mistakes are essential to the learning process and should be cast in a positive light. The focus should not be on whether the leader did well or poorly, but

FMFM 1-3 ——————— **Making It Happen**

on what progress he is making in his overall development as a leader. We must aim to provide the best climate to grow leaders. Damaging a leader's self-esteem, especially publicly, should be strictly avoided. A leader's self-confidence is the wellspring from which flows his willingness to assume responsibility and exercise initiative.

In that light, the greatest failing of a leader is a failure to act. A leader should assume great risk willingly. For him, two steadfast rules apply. First, in situations clearly requiring independent decisions, a leader has not only the latitude to make them, but the solemn duty to do so. This is an honorable effort to practice the art of warfighting. Second, inaction and omission — the antithesis of leadership — are much worse than judgmental error based on a sincere effort to act decisively. While errors in judgment might result in unsuccessful engagements, the broad exercise of initiative by all will likely carry the battle. Failure resulting from prudent risk taken by a thinking leader carries no disgrace since no single action guarantees success.

SUMMARY

Waging maneuver-style warfare demands a professional body of officers and men schooled in its science and art. As Marshal Foch said,

No study is possible on the battle-field; one does there simply what one can in order to apply what one knows. Therefore, in order to do even a little, one has already to know a great deal and know it well.[4]

Everything we do in peacetime should prepare us for combat. Our preparation for combat depends upon training and education which develop the action and thought essential to waging decisive battle.

Introduction

1. Sir William Slim, *Defeat into Victory* (London: Cassell and Co. Ltd., 1956), 550-551.

2. Charles Jean Jacques Joseph Ardant du Picq, *Battle Studies* (New York: MacMillan, 1921), 47.

3. D. K. Palit, *The Essentials of Military Knowledge* (Aldershot, England: Gale and Polden, 1947), xviii.

4. Freiherr Colmar von der Goltz, *Conduct of War* (Kansas City, MO: Franklin Hudson, 1896; reprint, Carlisle Barracks, PA: U.S. Army War College, 1983), vol. 51, *Art of War Colloquium*, 25.

5. Karl von Clausewitz, *On War* (Princeton University Press, 1984), 86.

6. B. L. Montgomery of Alamein, *A History of Warfare* (Cleveland, OH: World Publishing, 1968), 14.

7. J. B. Wheeler, *Art and Science of War* (New York: Van Nostrand, 1889), 9.

8. FMFM 1, *Warfighting*, 23.

Achieving a Decision

1. *Infantry in Battle*, 2d ed. (Richmond, VA: Garrett & Massie, 1939), 1.

2. Joint Pub 1-02: "**forward edge of the battle area** — (DOD, NATO) The foremost limits of a series of areas in which ground combat units are deployed, excluding the areas in which the covering or screening forces are operating, designated to coordinate fire support, the positioning of forces, or the maneuver units."

3. For an authoritative account of the battle of Antietam and its consequences, see:
James V. Murfin, *The Gleam of Bayonets* (Baton Rouge: Louisiana State University Press, 1965).

4. *Oxford English Dictionary* (U.K.: Oxford at the Clarendon Press, 1933), vol. II.

5. David G. Chandler, *The Campaigns of Napoleon* (New York: MacMillan, 1966), 15-28.

6. Robert A. Doughty, *The Breaking Point: Sedan and the Fall of France, 1940* (Hamden, CT: Archon Books, 1990), 266-270.

7. Attributed.

Gaining Leverage

1. Col. John C. Studt, USMC (Ret), "Foreword" in *Maneuver Warfare Handbook*, William S. Lind (Boulder, Colorado: Westview Press, 1985), xi.

2. Joint Pub 1-02: "**Maneuver**—(DOD, NATO) . . . 4. Employment of forces on the battlefield through movement in combination with fire, or fire potential, to achieve a position of advantage in respect to the enemy in order to accomplish the mission."

3. FMFM 1, *Warfighting*, 37.

4. Capt. B.H. Liddell-Hart, "The 'Man-in-the-Dark' Theory of Infantry Tactics and the 'Expanding Torrent' System of Attack," *Journal of the R.U.S.I.*, (February 1921), 13.

5. Erwin Rommel, *Attacks* (Vienna, VA: Athena Press, 1979), 235-250.

Trapping The Enemy

1. B. H. Liddell Hart, *Thoughts on War* (London: Faber & Faber, 1944), i.

2. F. Scott Fitzgerald, *Tender Is the Night* (New York: Charles Scribner, 1934), 56-57; quoted in Col. David Jablonsky, USA, *Churchill: The Making of a Grand Strategist* (Carlisle Barracks, PA: U.S. Army War College, 1990), 3.

3. For a comprehensive discussion of German tactical innovation during WWI, see:
B.I. Gudmundsson, *Stormtroop Tactics* (New York: Praeger, 1989).

4. *The Marines In Vietnam 1954-1973; An Anthology and Annotated Bibliography* (Washington, D.C.: Government Printing Office, 1985), 173-181.

5. Andre Laffargue, *Fantassin de Gascogne. De Mon Jardin a la Marne et au Danube* [Infantryman of Gascony. From my garden to the Marne and the Danube] (Paris: Elammarion, 1962), 59-78.
Mr. Laffargue presents one of the few personal accounts of small-unit tactics of WWI.

6. FMFM 1, *Warfighting*, 75.

7. FMFM 1, *Warfighting*, 6.

8. For a better understanding of the German perspective on the Battle of France and the thinking that entered into the final decisions, see:
Erich von Manstein, *Lost Victories* (Novato, CA: Presidio Press, 1982), ch. 5.

For a battalion-level account of the battle, see:
Hans von Luck, *Panzer Commander* (New York: Praeger, 1989), ch 7.

9. For further reading on the 1973 Arab-Israeli War, see:
Edgar O'Ballance, *No Victor, No Vanquished* (San Rafael, CA: Presidio Press, 1978).

Moving Faster

1. *Infantry in Battle*, 2d ed. (Richmond, VA: Garrett & Massie, 1939), 94.

2. Attributed.

3. Attributed.

4. Gen. Hermann Balck, interview by Wm. S. Lind, 6 June 1980, Washington, D.C.

5. Col. Ray Smith, USMC, telephone interview by Capt. S.R. Shoemaker, USMC, 12 March 1991, Washington, D.C.

6. Gen. Hermann Balck, interview by Wm. S. Lind, 6 June 1980, Washington, D.C.

7. Wm. S. Lind, *Maneuver Warfare Handbook* (Boulder, CO: Westview Press, 1985), 5-6.

8. George S. Patton, Jr., *War As I Knew It* (Boston: Houghton Mifflin, 1947), 341.

9. Charles Edward White, *The Enlightened Soldier* (New York: Praeger, 1989), 176.

10. Capt. A.T. Mahan, USN, *The Life of Nelson: The Embodiment of the Sea Power of Great Britain* (Boston: Little, Brown, and Co., 1899), 730.

11. *21.Pz.D., Ia, Anglage zum KTB Nr. 5, Gefechtsbericht III./Schuetz. Rgt. 104 (mot), 2.6.42*, U.S. Archives, German Records, Divisions, T-31.

Cooperation

1. NAVMC 7386, *Tactical Principles* (Quantico, VA: Marine Corps Schools, 1955), 7.

2. Panzermeyer (Kurt Meyer), *Grenadiere* (Munich: Schild Verlag, 1956), 196-201.
Mr. Paul Gartenmann of Arlington, Virginia, translated the passages.

Making It Happen

1. T. E. Lawrence, "The Science of Guerrilla Warfare," intro. to "Guerrilla Warfare," *Encyclopedia Britannica,* 13th ed. (New York: Encyclopedia Britannica, 1926).

2. As attibuted to Erwin Rommel by Robert Debs Heinl, Jr., *Dictionary of Military and Naval Quotations*, (Annapolis, MD: United States Naval Institute, 1985), 60.

3. George S. Patton, Jr., *War As I Knew It* (Boston: Houghton Mifflin, 1947), 354.

4. Ferdinand Foch, *The Principles of War*, trans. Hillaire Belloc (London: Chapman & Hall, 1920(?)), 5-6.

www.ingramcontent.com/pod-product-compliance
Lightning Source LLC
Chambersburg PA
CBHW030001050426
42451CB00006B/80